CATS ARE cool

SIAMESE

by Ruth Owen

PowerKiDS
press.

New York

Published in 2014 by The Rosen Publishing Group, Inc.
29 East 21st Street, New York, NY 10010

Produced for Rosen by Ruby Tuesday Books Ltd
Editor for Ruby Tuesday Books Ltd: Mark J. Sachner
US Editor: Sara Howell
Designer: Emma Randall

Photo Credits:
Cover, 1, 5, 6–7, 9, 10–11, 12–13, 14–15, 16–17, 18–19, 21, 22–23, 24–25, 27, 30 © Shutterstock; 8 ©
Public domain; 26 © www.siameserescue.org; 28 © Alamy; 29 © Rex Features.

Library of Congress Cataloging-in-Publication Data

Owen, Ruth, 1967–
 Siamese / By Ruth Owen.
    p. cm. — (Cats are cool)
 Includes index.
 ISBN 978-1-4777-1280-1 (library binding) — ISBN 978-1-4777-1346-4 (pbk.) —
 ISBN 978-1-4777-1347-1 (6-pack)
 1. Siamese cat—Juvenile literature. I. Title.
 SF449.S5O94 2014
 636.8'25—dc23
                                  2013006431

Manufactured in the United States of America

CPSIA Compliance Information: Batch #: S13PK7 For Further Information contact: Rosen Publishing, New York, New York at 1-800-237-9932

Contents

Marvelous Meezers

What is extremely smart, has a sleek, silky body, beautiful blue eyes, and just loves to talk or meow with its owner? The answer is a Siamese cat.

There are many different types, or **breeds**, of cats in the world. A **purebred** cat has **ancestors** that all came from the same breed. So its parents, grandparents, great-grandparents, and so on, all looked similar.

Siamese cats are purebred cats. They are one of the oldest cat breeds that people know about. In fact, these cats have been around for so long that no one can even say how or when the breed got started.

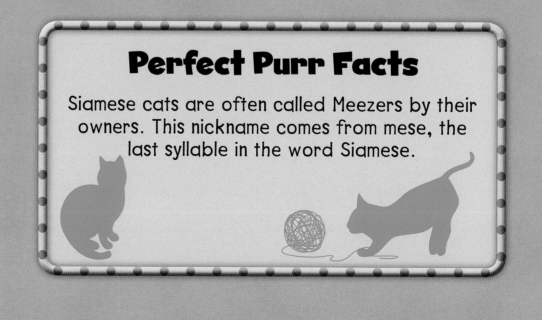

Perfect Purr Facts

Siamese cats are often called Meezers by their owners. This nickname comes from mese, the last syllable in the word Siamese.

A Siamese kitten

5

Cool Cat Legends

The history of Siamese cats is lost in time. We do know, however, that they came from Siam, a country in Asia. Today, Siam is called Thailand.

When travelers to Siam brought back cats to countries such as Britain and the United States, **legends** about the cats came, too. Some old stories said that Siamese cats lived in temples. Others said that the cats were the favorites of royalty and important, **noble** families.

One legend said that when a person from a noble family died, his or her **spirit** would continue living inside the body of one of the family's Siamese cats. The cat would then go to live in a temple. Here, the cat would live in luxury, cared for by servants and the temple priests!

A Siamese cat

Perfect Purr Facts

A white cat with a black face, ears, paws, and tail appears in poems known as Tamra Maew, or Cat Poems. The poems are from Thailand and are hundreds of years old.

A temple in modern-day Thailand

The First Siamese

Just like her royal ancestors, the first Siamese cat to come to the United States from Thailand had very important owners. She belonged to President Rutherford B. Hayes and the First Lady, Lucy Hayes!

President Rutherford B. Hayes

In 1878, David B. Sickels, a United States government official, was living and working in Bangkok, the capital of Thailand. When he discovered that the First Lady was a cat lover, he arranged for one of the beautiful cats he'd seen in Thailand to be sent to the White House.

Siam, the White House Siamese, was much loved by the first family and their staff. In 1879, however, Siam suddenly fell ill. Even the president's personal doctor couldn't help the little Siamese, and sadly, she died.

The White House

Perfect Purr Facts

Siam was not the Rutherford family's only pet. She shared the job of "First Pet" with two dogs, a goat, and a mockingbird.

Pho and Mia

In 1884, Edward Gould, a British government official who worked in Bangkok, brought two Siamese cats back to Britain from Thailand.

The male and female cats were named Pho, which means "father," and Mia, which means "mother." Pho and Mia had kittens together, and the cat family was shown off at a cat show in London.

In the 1800s, most cats in Britain had sturdy bodies with round faces. Pho, Mia, and their kittens were slim and sleek, with triangle-shaped faces. When visitors to the cat show saw the Siamese cats, they became very excited about this **exotic** new breed.

During the 1800s, most British cats looked like the cats in this photo.

Perfect Purr Facts

In the late 1800s, Siamese cats in Britain were known as "The Royal Cats of Siam." Today, however, no one knows if Siamese cats really were owned and **bred** by royalty in their home country.

People were fascinated by Siamese cats when they first appeared in British cat shows in the late 1800s.

The Siamese Look

When American, British, and European cat lovers first saw Siamese cats in the 1800s, most loved the look of the unusual cats.

The cats had large ears and long faces, or snouts. When viewed from the front, the cat's snout and ears created a triangle shape.

The cats had long, muscular bodies with long necks and legs. They also had long, whiplike tails that got thinner toward the tips.

The only thing that wasn't long about the Siamese cats was their short, silky fur. The shortness of the fur helped show off their slim, athletic bodies.

Short fur

Long legs and tail

Large ears

Perfect Purr Facts

All Siamese cats have blue, almond-shaped eyes that slant toward their noses.

Blue eyes

Triangle-shaped face

Siamese Colors

Cat lovers in the 1800s weren't only excited about the shape of Siamese cats. They also loved the cats' pale coat colors and dark markings.

Siamese cats have markings, called **points**, that are darker than their main body color. There are four main Siamese color combinations. These are seal point, chocolate point, blue point, and lilac point.

Seal point Siamese cats have a **fawn**, or cream, body with brown, almost black, points. Chocolate point Siamese have an **ivory**-colored body with points that are the color of chocolate.

Blue point Siamese cats aren't really blue. They have a grayish-white body and dark gray points. Lilac point Siamese have a white body with pale, pinkish-gray points.

Chocolate point
Siamese cat

Blue point
Siamese cat

Seal point
Siamese cat

Perfect Purr Facts

The dark points, or markings, on a Siamese cat cover its face, ears, feet or feet and legs, and its tail.

Lilac point Siamese cat

15

Different Looks, Still Beautiful!

After the first Siamese cats were brought from Thailand to North America and Europe, the breed quickly became very popular.

Many people wanted to own one of the unusual-looking Siamese cats. So, cat breeders began breeding more and more Siamese cats.

Some breeders bred cats with the original slim, long shape and pointed color pattern. Other breeders cared only about breeding kittens that had the Siamese colors and markings. These breeders sometimes mated Siamese cats with non-Siamese cats. This created cats with Siamese coloring, but heavier bodies and more rounded faces.

Today, it's possible to see Siamese cats with both looks. Breeders don't always agree about which look is a true Siamese cat, but most owners don't mind. They just love their beautiful pet cats!

This adult seal point Siamese cat has the more rounded shape and face.

Perfect Purr Facts

Siamese cats that compete in cat shows usually have the long, slim body shape and triangle-shaped head.

These Siamese kittens have the long, slim look.

A Feline Friend for Life

No matter what their Siamese cats look like, owners all agree that these cats make wonderful feline friends.

Siamese are very **inquisitive** and love to investigate new things. They also love to play with toys and will happily play for hours at a time, even when they get older.

Siamese cats are very loving and form strong **bonds** with their owners. They love to sit on their owners' laps, follow them around, and snuggle up under the quilt at night.

If a Siamese cat is left alone or ignored, however, it will become very unhappy. So Siamese cats need owners who can give them lots of time and attention.

Perfect Purr Facts

Like a dog, a Siamese cat will play fetch with its owner. If you throw a toy for a Siamese cat, it will fetch the toy and jump up into your lap to return it!

This is my favorite toy!

I'm a Siamese. Playing is what I do best!

Something Important to Say!

Siamese cats love being around people. One of the ways they show how much they love their human family and friends is by making noise!

Siamese cats communicate with their owners using loud meows that often sound like a baby crying. Owners say that when they get home from school or work, their Siamese cats seem to be itching to tell them all about their day in loud meows.

If you ask a Siamese cat a question, it will always answer you. You won't understand what the cat's meow means. That won't stop a Siamese from being sure that what it has to say is very, very important, though!

Perfect Purr Facts

Siamese cats aren't just loving to humans. They also form strong bonds with other cats and even dogs. People with several Siamese cats often find their loving pets cuddled up together asleep in a big, tangled heap.

A Newborn Siamese Kitten

When a Siamese kitten is born, it is completely white. Its eyes are closed and its little ears are folded down.

The kitten's body can't stay warm on its own, so it cuddles up to its mother for warmth. Along with its brothers and sisters, a newborn kitten spends all its time sleeping or drinking milk from its mother.

In its second week the kitten's eyes will open. Then, when it is three weeks old, its ears will unfold and stand up straight. At this age, it might also be possible to see the kitten's dark points appearing on its nose, paws, and tail.

A Siamese cat feeding her kittens

A mother Siamese
cat and her
newborn kittens

Perfect Purr Facts

A newborn Siamese kitten weighs between
3 and 5 ounces (85–142 g). That's less
than a baseball!

Little Siamese

At four to five weeks old, a Siamese kitten will be able to walk, and it will begin to play and explore.

At this age, the kitten will still drink its mother's milk, but it will also start to eat canned kitten food.

These Siamese kittens are 10 weeks old. Their points are growing darker and can now be easily seen.

24

At eight weeks old, a kitten will be racing around the house playing with its brothers and sisters. If the kitten belongs to a cat breeder, the breeder will spend time petting and playing with the kitten so it is not scared of people.

By the time it is 12 weeks old, a kitten will be large enough and brave enough to leave its mother and go to live in a new home.

Perfect Purr Facts

Before a kitten goes to its new owner, a breeder will train it to go to the bathroom in a **litter box**. The breeder will also take the kitten to a veterinarian to have **vaccinations** that will protect it from diseases.

The Meezer Express

Some people buy their Siamese cat from a breeder. Others choose their cat from a **rescue shelter**. One such shelter, the Siamese Cat Rescue Center in Virginia, takes care of homeless Siamese cats and tries to find them new owners.

Sometimes people who want a Siamese cat live hundreds of miles (km) from the rescue center and have no way of picking up their new pet. Then the Siamese may travel to its new home on the *Meezer Express*. The *Meezer Express* is organized by drivers who give up their free time to help cats. If a Siamese has to travel a long distance, several people each drive part of the trip. Just like in a relay race, the cat is passed from driver to driver.

Finally, thanks to the *Meezer Express*, the lucky Siamese arrives at its new forever home!

Cars taking part in the *Meezer Express* display this sign.

I'm going home!

meezer express
WWW.SIAMESERESCUE.ORG

Perfect Purr Facts

A cat may be homeless because its owner has died or can no longer afford to care for it. Sadly, some people decide they no longer want their Siamese cat because it needs too much care and attention.

Meezers travel to their new homes in comfortable cat carriers that contain a litter box.

Siamese Cats in the Movies

Siamese cats have appeared in many books, movies, and TV shows, including the Disney movie *Lady and the Tramp*.

When Lady's owners go on a trip, Aunt Sarah arrives to take care of the house and the family's baby son. Unfortunately, Aunt Sarah brings her two singing Siamese cats, Si and Am, with her.

Si and Am immediately cause trouble, tearing the curtains and trying to eat the pet canary and fish. Having caused havoc in the house, Si and Am then pretend it was Lady that did all the damage!

The Siamese cats in Disney's movie may have been the bad guys, but it's just a movie. Meezer owners know these loving, talkative, beautiful felines are real good guys and the coolest cats around!

Lady, the cocker spaniel, with Si and Am, the naughty Siamese.

Bodger, Luath, and Tao the Siamese cat in *The Incredible Journey*.

Perfect Purr Facts

In the book and movie *The Incredible Journey*, two dogs and a Siamese cat are separated from their owners. The pets have to cross 250 miles (400 km) of Canadian **wilderness** to be reunited with their family.

Glossary

ancestors (AN-ses-terz) A relative that lived long ago.

bonds (BONDZ) A close connection based on love and trust.

bred (BRED) Put together two animals to mate and produce young.

breeds (BREEDS) A type of cat or other animal. Also, the word used to describe the act of mating two animals in order to produce young.

exotic (ek-ZAH-tik) Unusual, different, or from a foreign country.

fawn (FAHN) A very pale brown, like the color of a fawn, or baby deer.

feline (FEE-lyn) A cat or other member of the cat family, such as a lion or a tiger.

inquisitive (in-KWIH-zih-tiv) Curious and nosy.

ivory (EYEV-ree) A creamy-white color.

legends (LEH-jendz) A story handed down over the years that may be based on some facts but cannot be proven to be true.

litter box (LIH-ter BOKS) A shallow plastic box or tray filled with stony or sandy material that a cat uses as a bathroom.

noble (NOH-bul) Important and high ranking.

points (POYNTZ) The colored face, tail, feet, legs, and ears of a cat with a light body.

purebred (PYUHR-bred) An animal whose parents and ancestors were all bred from members of one breed.

rescue shelter (RES-kyoo SHEL-ter) A place where people take unwanted pets. Workers at a shelter care for the animals and try to find them a new home.

spirit (SPIR-ut) Believed to be the energy or life-force inside a living thing.

vaccinations (vak-suh-NAY-shuhnz) Medicine that is usually given as a shot to protect animals and people against diseases.

wilderness (WIL-dur-nis) A wild area where there are no towns or cities.

Websites

Due to the changing nature of Internet links, PowerKids Press has developed an online list of websites related to the subject of this book. This site is updated regularly. Please use this link to access the list:

www.powerkidslinks.com/cac/siam/

Read More

Landau, Elaine. *Siamese Are the Best!*. Best Cats Ever. Minneapolis, MN: Lerner Publishing Group, 2011.

Mattern, Joanne. *Siamese Cats*. All About Cats. Mankato, MN: Capstone Press, 2011.

White, Nancy. *Siamese: Talk to Me!*. Cat-ographies. New York: Bearport Publishing, 2011.

Index